Fisher-Price TODDLER LEARNING PAD

ALL SET TO DISCOVER

MODERN PUBLISHING
A Division of Unisystems, Inc.
New York, New York 10022
Printed in the U.S.A
Series UPC: 49415

Copyright ©1998, 2000, 2002, 2003 Modern Publishing, a division of Unisystems, Inc.

Fisher-Price, Little People, and related trademarks, copyrights, and character designs
are used under license from Fisher-Price, Inc., a subsidiary of Mattel, Inc.,
East Aurora, NY 14052 U.S.A. ©1998, 2000, 2002, 2003 Mattel, Inc. All Rights Reserved.
MADE IN THE U.S.A.
Manufactured for and distributed by Modern Publishing,
a division of Unisystems, Inc., New York, New York 10022

®Honey Bear Books is a trademark owned by Honey Bear Productions, Inc.,
and is registered in the U.S. Patent and Trademark Office.
No part of this book may be reproduced or copied in any form
without written permission from the publisher.
All Rights Reserved.

Printed in the U.S.A.

NOTE TO PARENTS

Dear Parents:

Helping your children master their world through early learning is as easy as the Fisher-Price® Learning Pads!

As your child's first and most important teacher, you can encourage his or her love of learning by participating in learning activities at home. Working together on the activities in each of the Fisher-Price® Toddler Learning Pads will help your child gain confidence and develop learning skills that will be crucial as he or she grows and begins school.

Help make your time together enjoyable and rewarding by following these suggestions:

- Choose a quiet time when you and your child are relaxed.
- Provide a selection of writing tools (pens, pencils, crayons).
- Discuss every page. Help you child relate the concepts in the book to everyday experiences.
- Only work on a few pages at a time. Don't attempt to complete every page if your child becomes tired or loses interest.
- Praise your child's efforts.

This title, All Set to Discover, teaches the following essential skills:
√ practicing fine motor skills and eye/hand coordination
√ using visual perception and visual discrimination skills
√ noticing similarities and differences
√ making comparisons
√ developing vocabulary skills
√ identifying colors and shapes
√ recognizing letters and numbers

Collect the entire series of Fisher-Price® Toddler Learning Pads:

- All Set to Learn
- All Set for Fun
- All Set to Think
- All Set to Discover

Can you match each picture to its shadow?
Can you make a hand shadow on the wall?

Skills: Visual discrimination; Visual perception; Skills

©1998 Fisher-Price, Inc.

Can you match each picture to its shadow?
Can you find your shadow on the ground?

Skills: Visual discrimination; Visual perception; Skills

©1998 Fisher-Price, Inc.

Roar Like a Lion!

Can you color the chair **blue**?
Can you color the table **yellow**?
Can you color the lamp **red**?
Can you name the colors on your furniture?

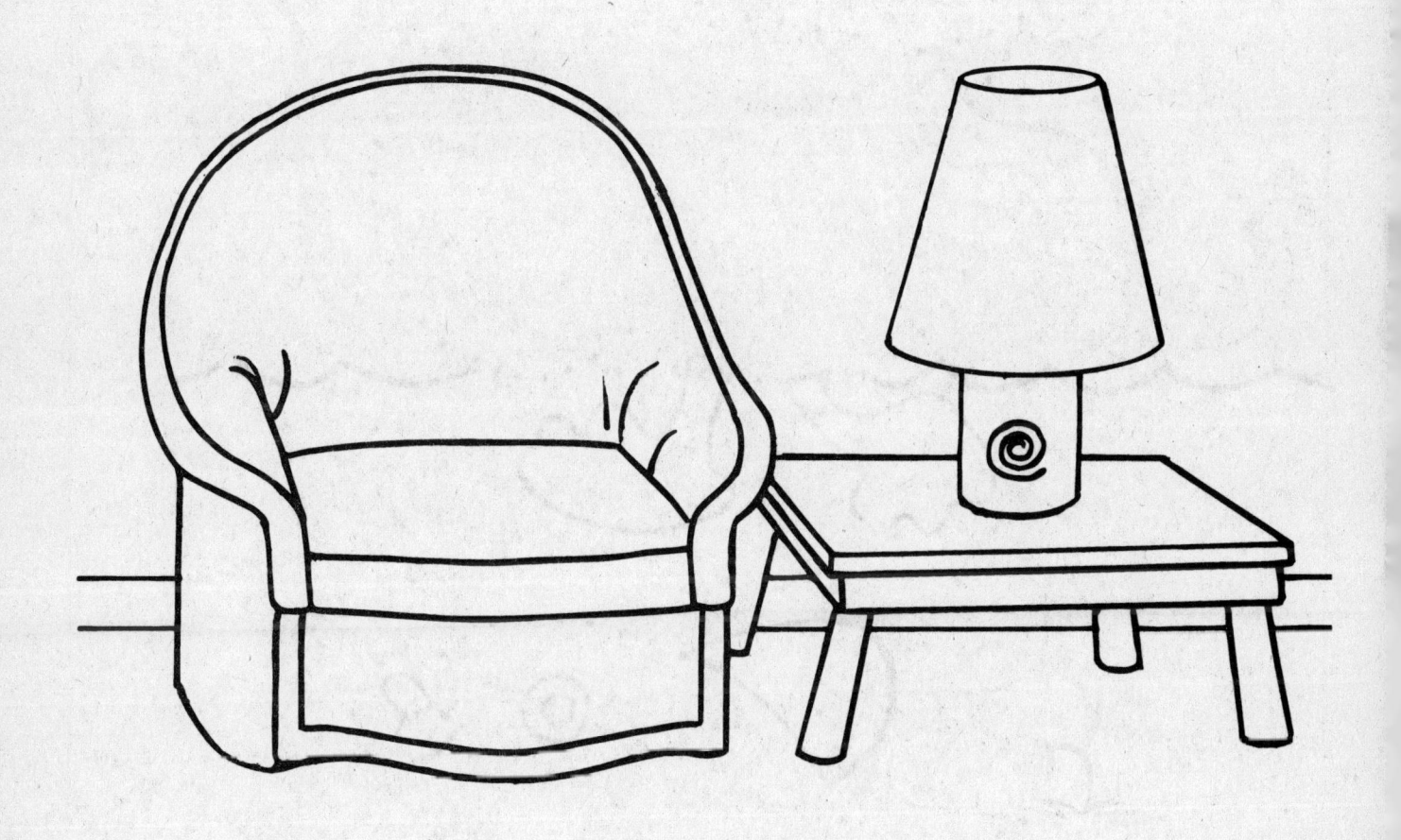

Skills: Understanding colors; Identifying objects; Extending vocabulary

Trace the animals on this page.
Can you color the duck **yellow**?
Can you color the fish **green**?
Can you name other animals that are **yellow** or **green**?

Skills: Understanding colors; Identifying objects; Extending vocabulary

Can you color the top **circle** in **red**?
Can you trace the bottom **circle** in **red**?
Can you find something **red** or something that is a **circle**?

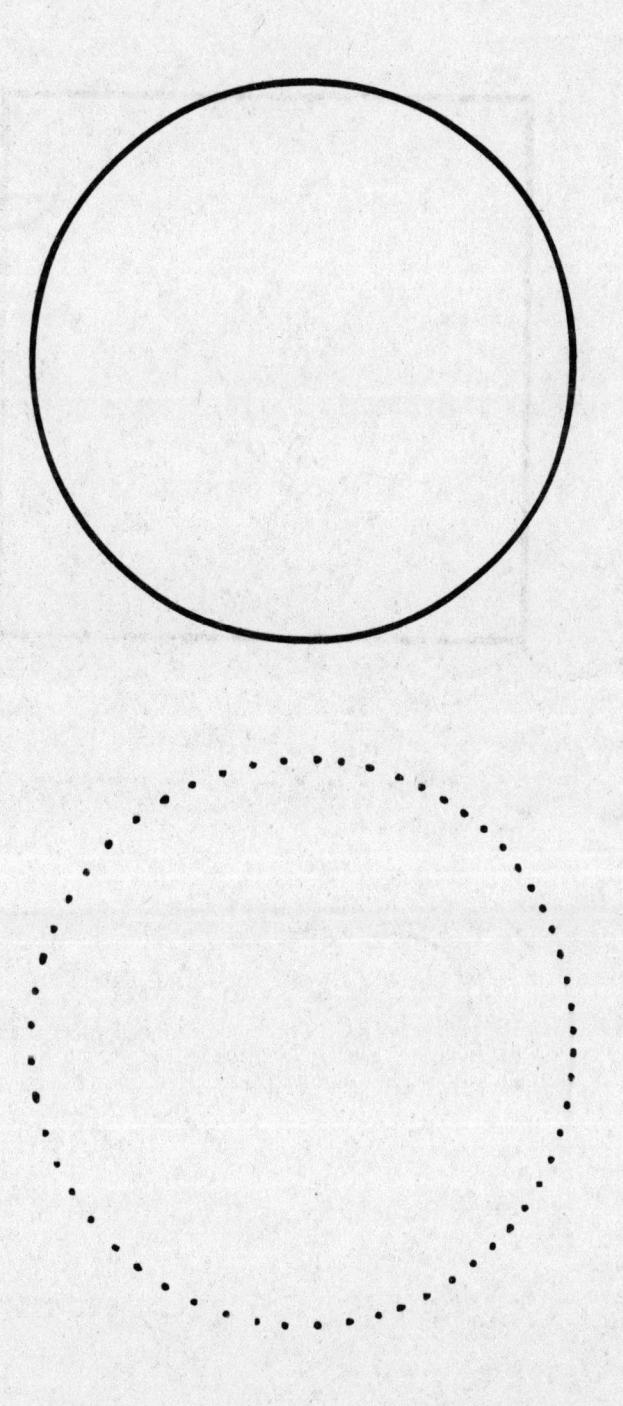

Skills: Understanding colors; Identifying shapes; Fine motor coordination skills; Following directions

©1998 Fisher-Price, Inc.

Can you color the top **square** in **blue**?
Can you trace the bottom **square** in **blue**?
Can you find something **blue** or something that is a **square**?

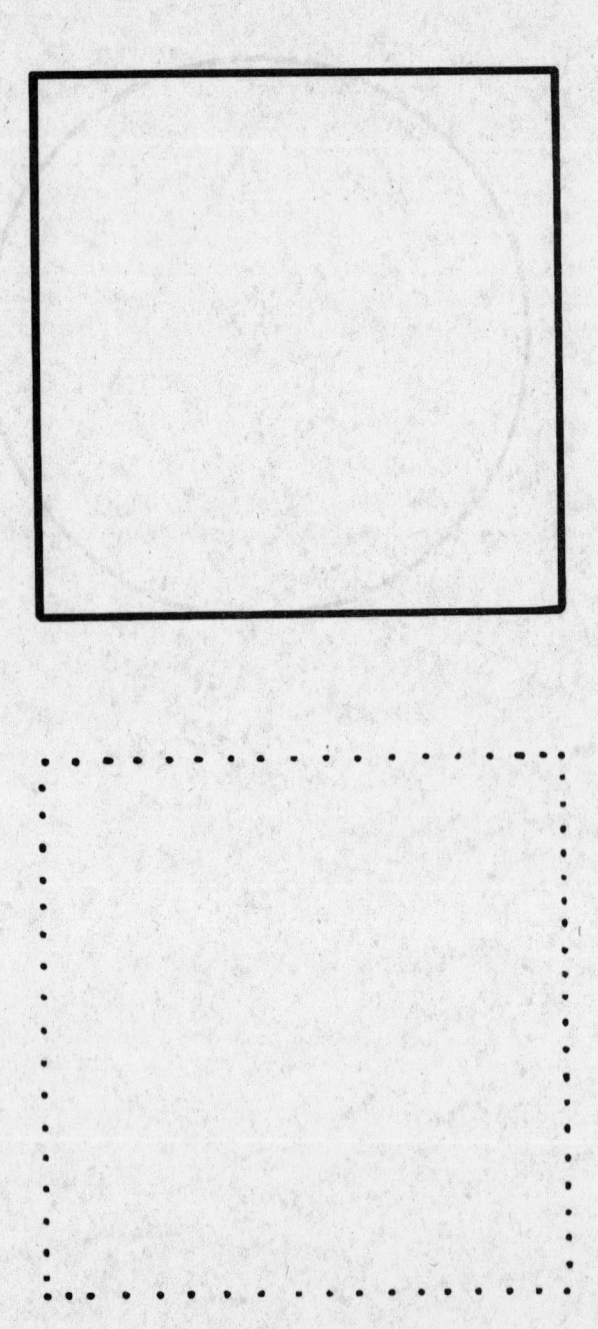

Skills: Understanding colors; Identifying shapes; Fine motor coordination skills; Following directions

Can you color the top **triangle** in **yellow**?
Can you trace the bottom **triangle** in **yellow**?
Can you find something **yellow** or something that is a **triangle**?

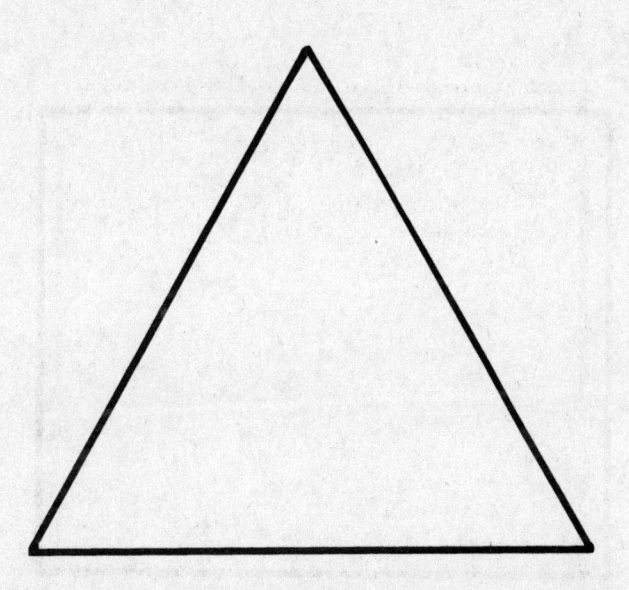

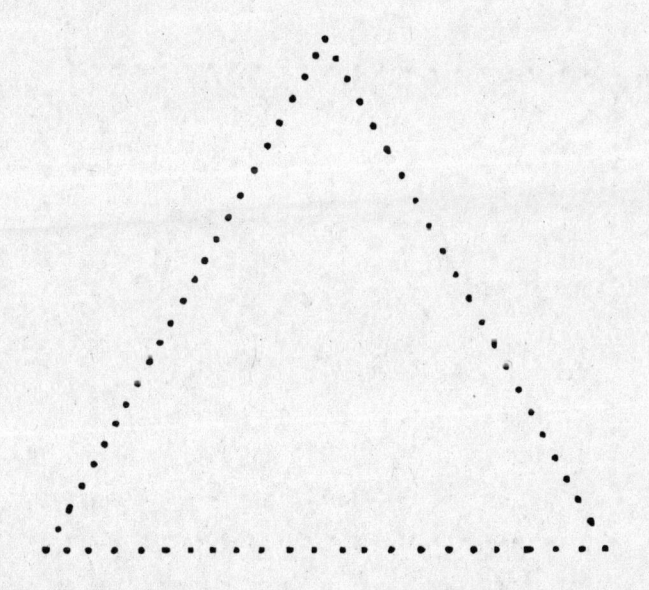

Skills: Understanding colors; Identifying shapes; Fine motor coordination skills; Following directions

©1998 Fisher-Price, Inc.

Can you color the top **rectangle** in **green**?
Can you trace the bottom **rectangle** in **green**?
Can you find something **green** or something that is a **rectangle**?

Skills: Understanding colors; Identifying shapes; Fine motor coordination skills; Following directions

Can you color the top **oval** in **orange**?
Can you trace the bottom **oval** in **orange**?
Can you find something **orange** or something that is an **oval**?

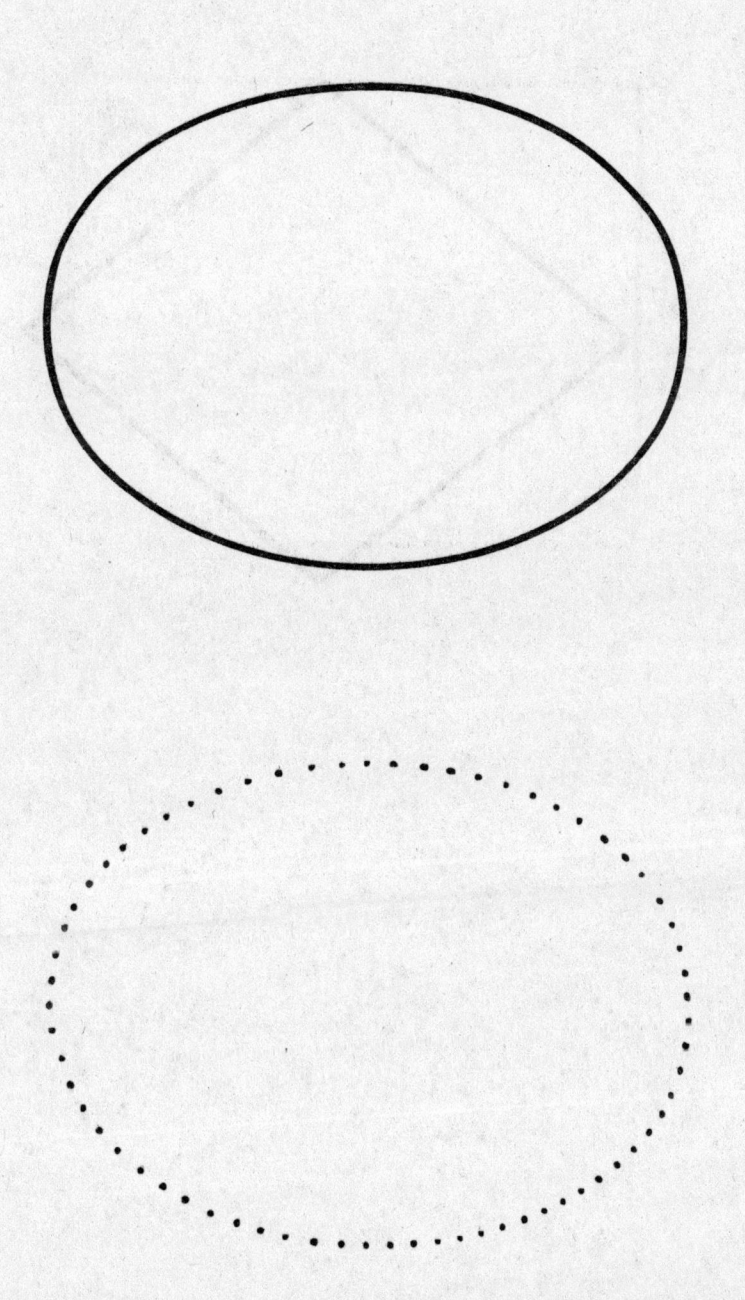

Skills: Understanding colors; Identifying shapes; Fine motor coordination skills; Following directions

Can you color the top **diamond** in **purple**?
Can you trace the bottom **diamond** in **purple**?
Can you find something **purple** or something that is a **diamond**?

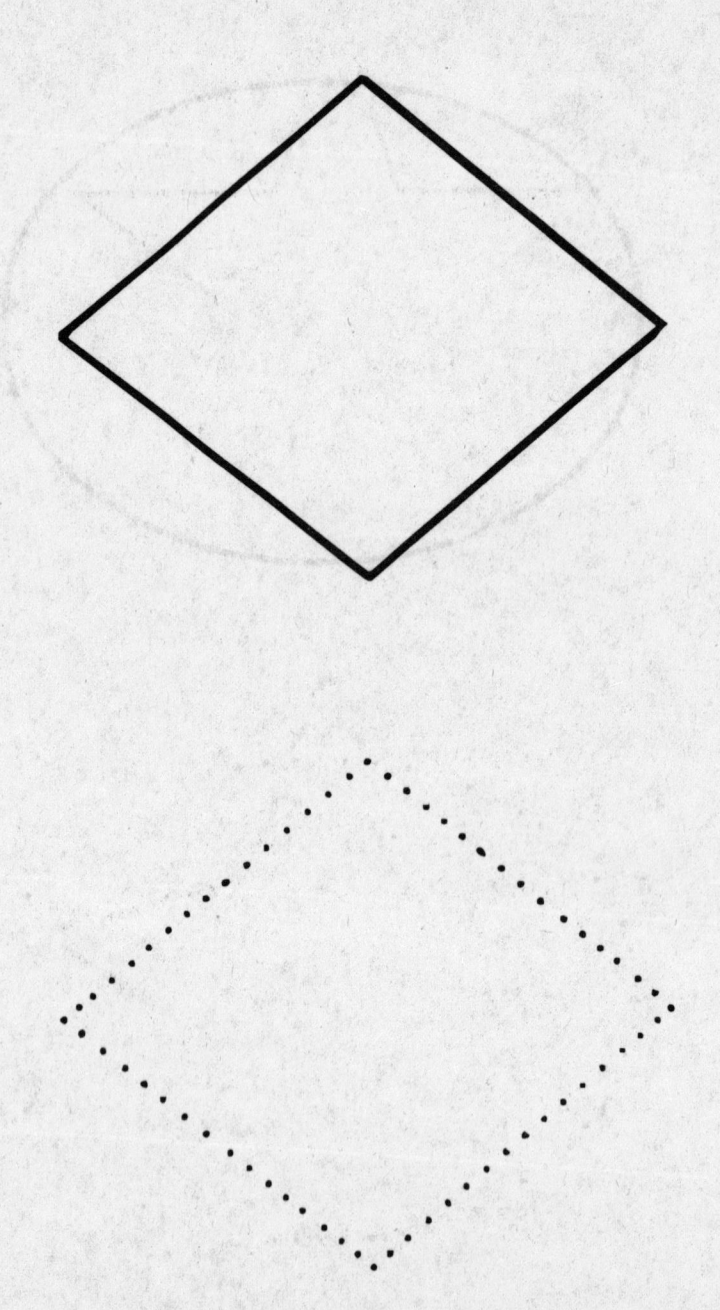

Skills: Understanding colors; Identifying shapes; Fine motor coordination skills; Following directions

Can you color the top **star** in **brown**?
Can you trace the bottom **star** in **brown**?
Can you find something **brown** or something that is a **star**?

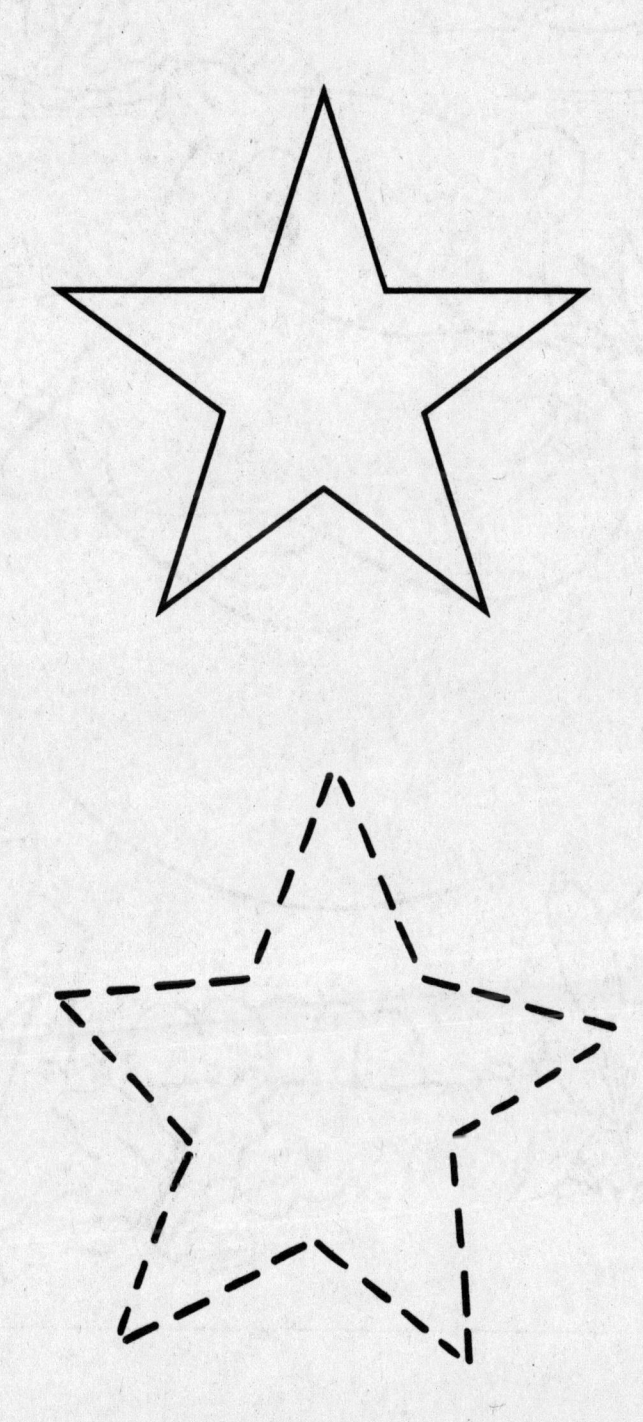

Skills: Understanding colors; Identifying shapes; Fine motor coordination skills; Following directions

The Happy Hippo!

Can you match the shapes that look the **same**?
Can you find matching shapes around you?

Skills: Matching shapes; Visual perception skills; Logical thinking

Can you count to **10** and follow the dots?
Then color the picture.
Can you clap your hands **10** times?

Skills: Recognizing numbers; Number order

Can you trace the lines to match things from the garden?
Then color the pictures.
Can you pretend to pick some flowers?

Skills: Fine motor skills; Eye/hand coordination

Can you name the letters and follow the dots?
Then color the picture.
Can you name each letter?

Skills: Recognizing letters; Letter order

Can you name the letters starting with **N** and follow the dots?
Then color the picture.
Can you name each letter?

Skills: Recognizing letters; Letter order

©1998 Fisher-Price, Inc.

21

Read about your favorite animal!

Can you tell what this picture really shows?
Then color the pictures.
Can you draw a picture and cut it up to make a puzzle?

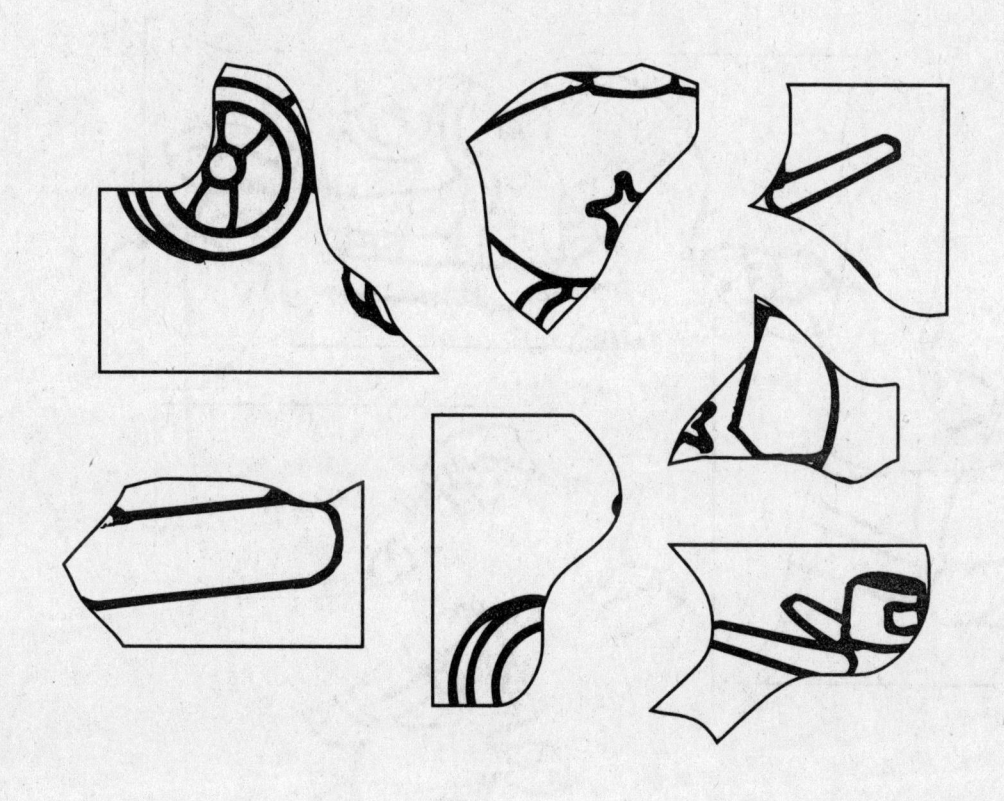

Skills: Visual discrimination; Visual perception

©1998 Fisher-Price, Inc.

Can you tell what this picture really shows?
Then color the pictures.
Can you cut up a magazine picture to make a puzzle?

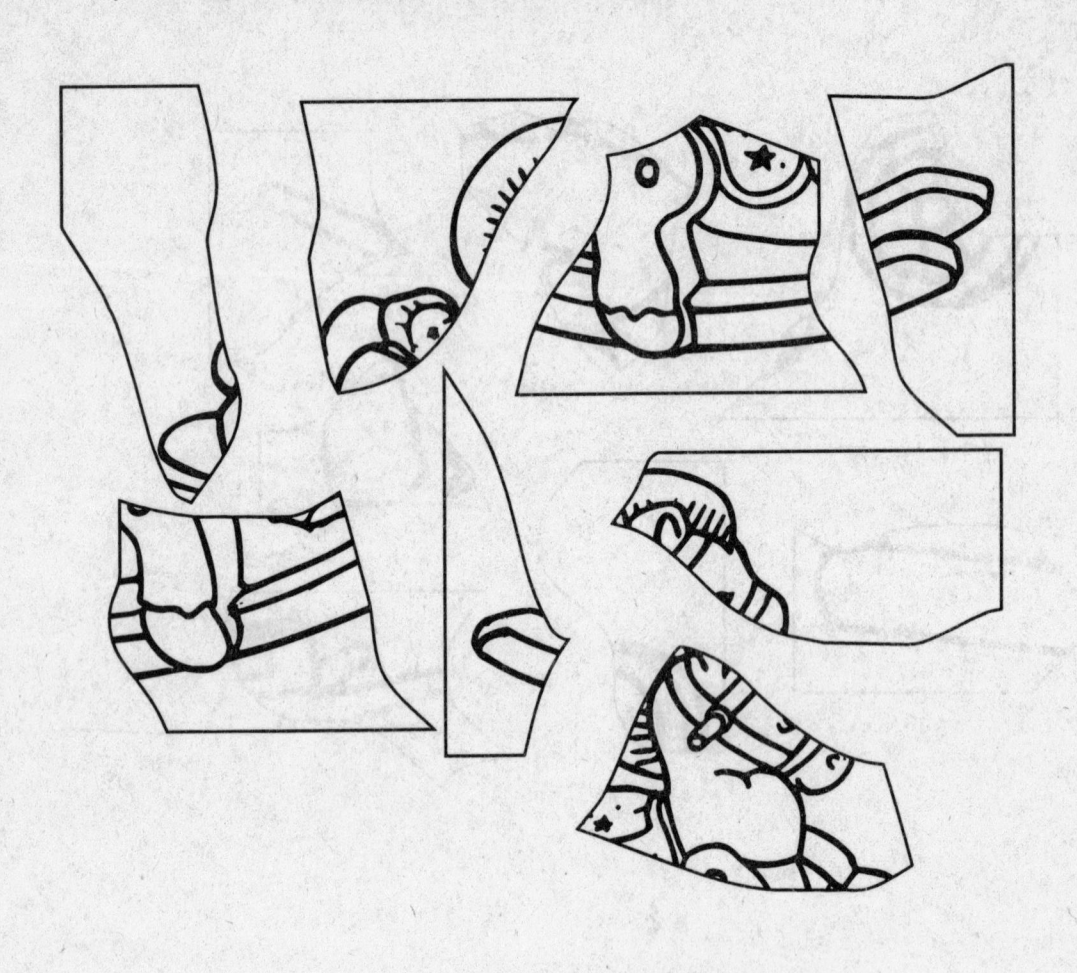

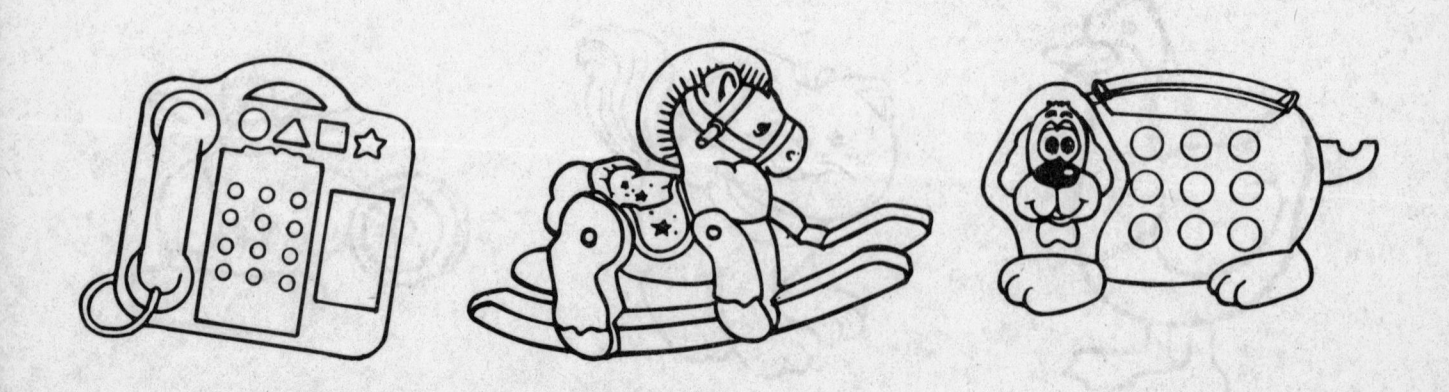

Skills: Visual discrimination; Visual perception

Can you color the picture that takes more time to do?
Can you think of something that takes a long time to do?

Skills: Awareness of time; Logical thinking

©1998 Fisher-Price, Inc.

Can you remember the animals on this page?
Color them and then flip the page.
Can you name animals that swim in the water?

Skills: Visual memory; Association; Following directions

Can you remember the animals from the last page?
Color the ones you remember.
Can you close your eyes and remember what you are wearing?

Skills: Visual memory; Association; Following directions

Jump like a monkey!

Can you circle someone holding a baby?
Can you circle someone holding a leash?
Then color the picture.
Can you find a kitten?

Skills: Noticing details; Following directions

Can you color the highest balloon **yellow**?
Can you color the lowest balloon **red**?
Can you color the balloon in the middle **blue**?

Skills: Recognizing position; Vocabulary development; Following directions

Can you circle the acorn at the **top**?
Can you draw a line under the acorn at the **bottom**?
Can you color the acorn in the **middle**?
What animals live in a tree?

Skills: Recognizing position; Vocabulary development; Following directions

Can you match the blocks that show the same letters?
Then color the picture.
Can you name the shapes of each block?

Skills: Visual matching; Letter recognition; Shape recognition

Can you color the fruits that show the same letters?
Can you name other kinds of fruits?

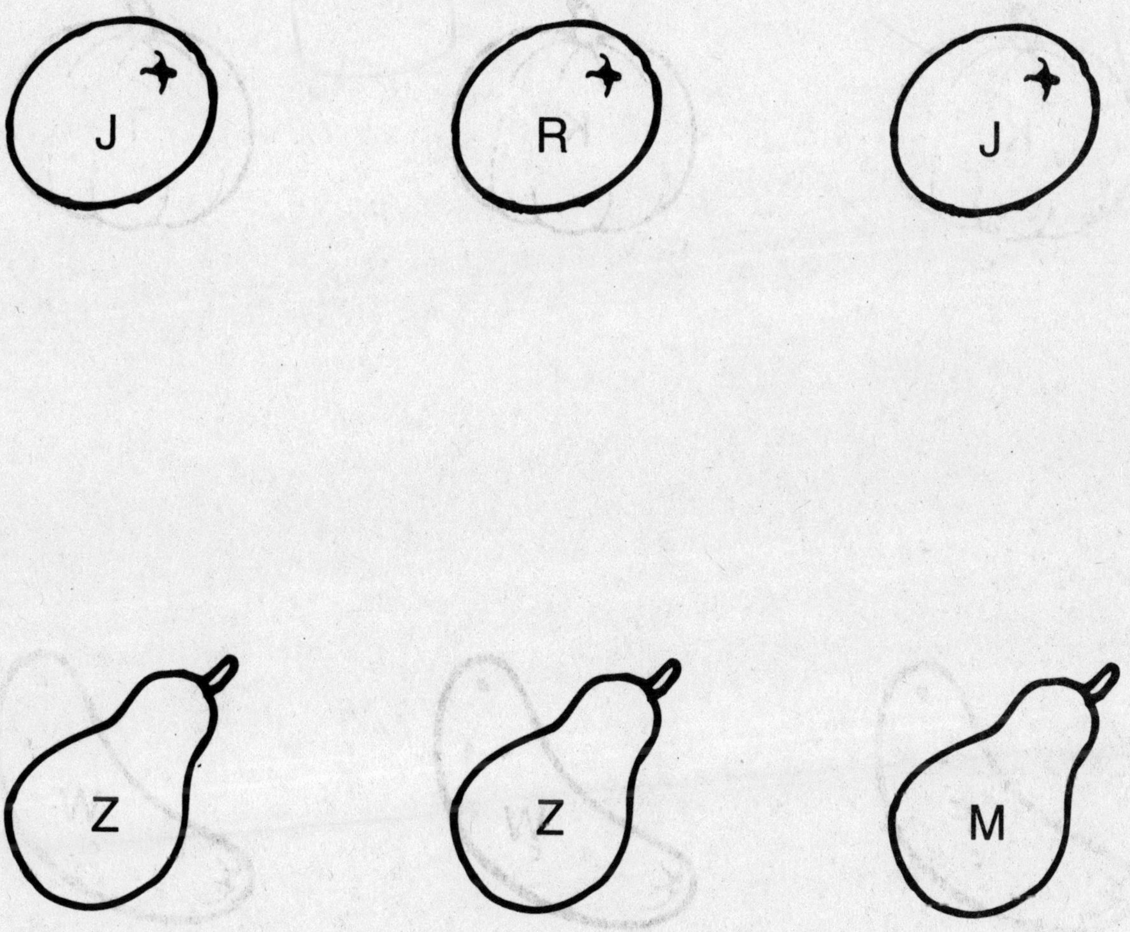

Skills: Visual matching; Letter recognition; Vocabulary development

Can you color the vegetables that show the same letters?
Can you name other kinds of vegetables?

K   K   T

F   W   W

Skills: Visual matching; Letter recognition; Vocabulary development

Can you color the leaves that show the same letters?
Can you pretend to be a falling leaf?

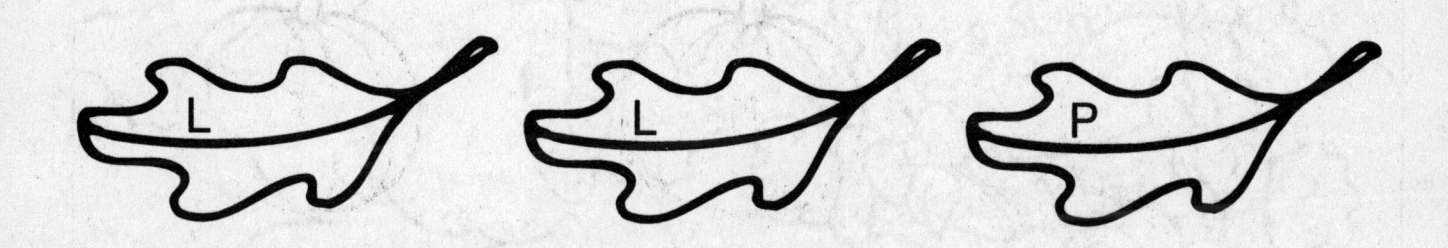

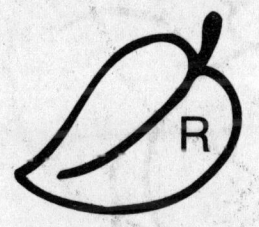

Skills: Visual matching; Letter recognition; Vocabulary development

Pretend to take a picture!

Can you color the matching number of things in each row?
Where could you use these things?

1	
2	
3	
4	
5	

Skills: Recognizing numbers; Creating sets of numbers

Can you color the matching number of things in each row?
Where could you find these things in your home?

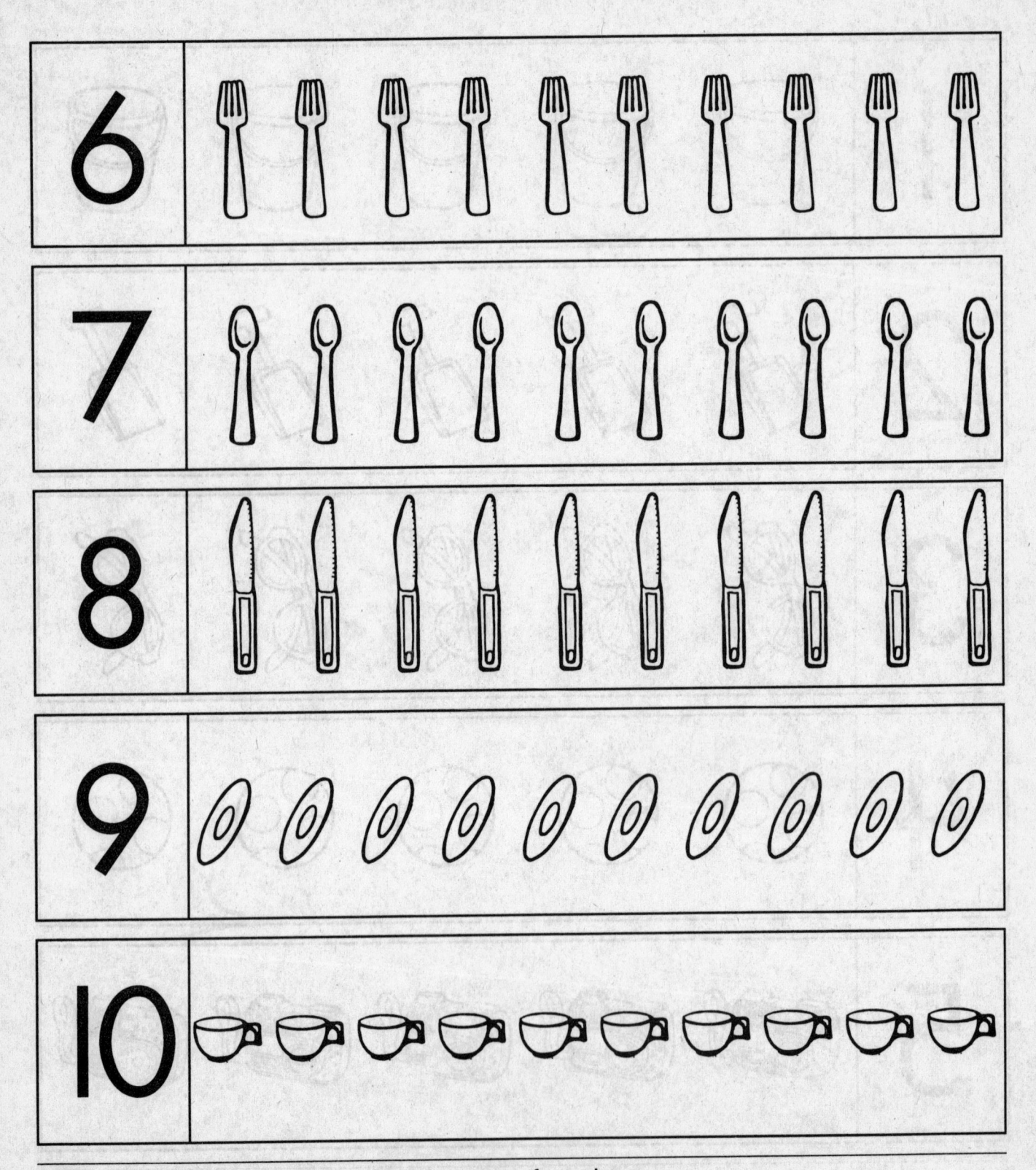

6

7

8

9

10

Skills: Recognizing numbers; Creating sets of numbers

Can you circle all the numbers?
Can you count to 5?

Skills: Recognizing numbers; Visual discrimination

©1998 Fisher-Price, Inc.

39

Can you mark the one that doesn't belong?
Then color the other pictures.
Why do they go together?

Skills: Association; Classification; Logical reasoning

©1998 Fisher-Price, Inc.

40

Can you mark the one that doesn't belong?
Then color the other pictures.
Why do they go together?

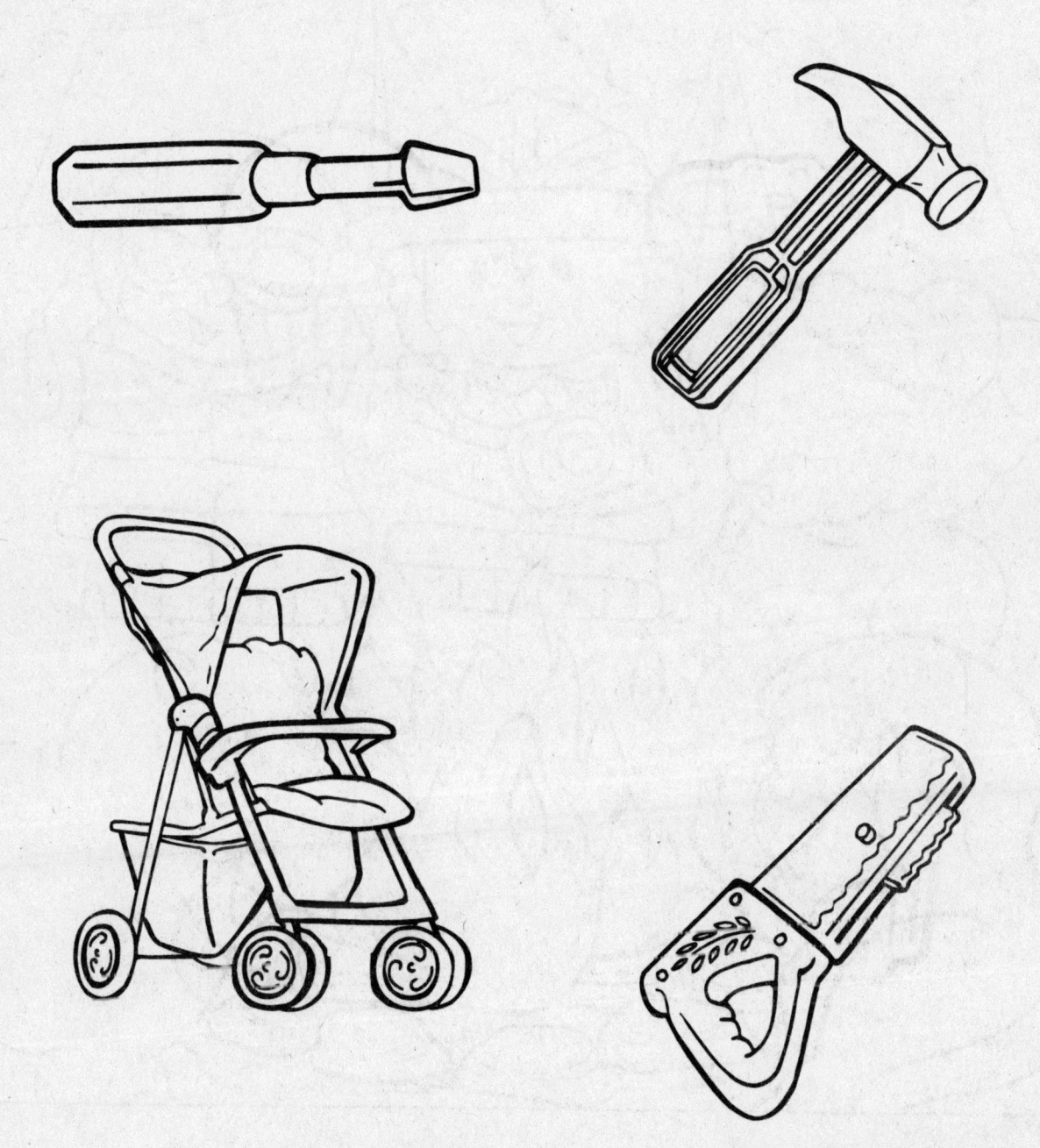

Skills: Association; Classification; Logical reasoning

It's fun to make a tent!

ANSWER KEY

Page 4
Can you match each picture to its shadow?
Can you make a hand shadow on the wall?

Page 7
Can you color the chair blue?
Can you color the table yellow?
Can you color the lamp red?
Can you name the colors on your furniture?

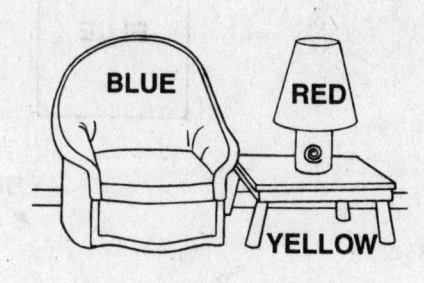

BLUE RED YELLOW

Page 5
Can you match each picture to its shadow?
Can you find your shadow on the ground?

Page 8
Can you color the duck yellow?
Can you color the fish green?
Can you name other animals that are yellow or green?

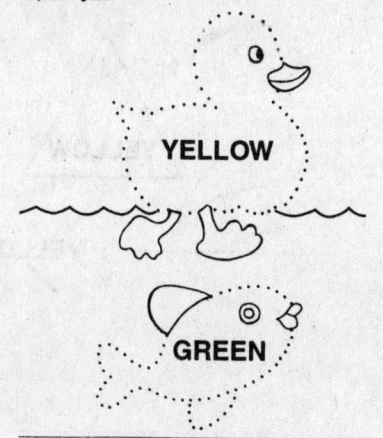

YELLOW GREEN

©1998 Fisher-Price, Inc.

43

ANSWER KEY

Page 9
Can you color the top circle in red?
Can you trace the bottom circle in red?
Can you find something red or something that is a circle?

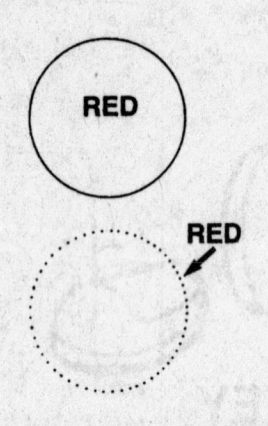

RED

RED

Page 10
Can you color the top square in blue?
Can you trace the bottom square in blue?
Can you find something blue or something that is a square?

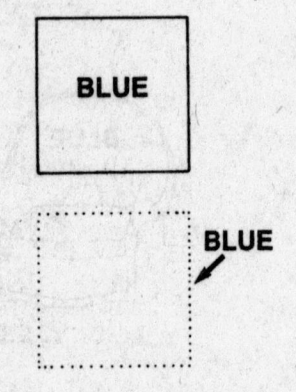

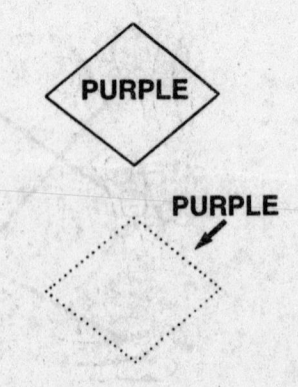

BLUE

BLUE

Page 11
Can you color the top triangle in yellow?
Can you trace the bottom triangle in yellow?
Can you find something yellow or something that is a triangle?

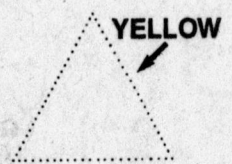

YELLOW

YELLOW

Page 12
Can you color the top rectangle in green?
Can you trace the bottom rectangle in green?
Can you find something green or something that is a rectangle?

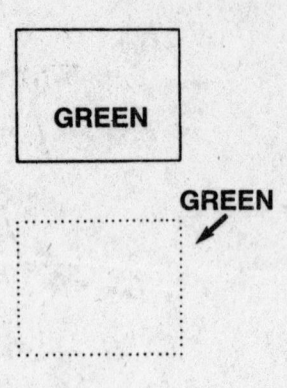

GREEN

GREEN

Page 13
Can you color the top oval in orange?
Can you trace the bottom oval in orange?
Can you find something orange or something that is an oval?

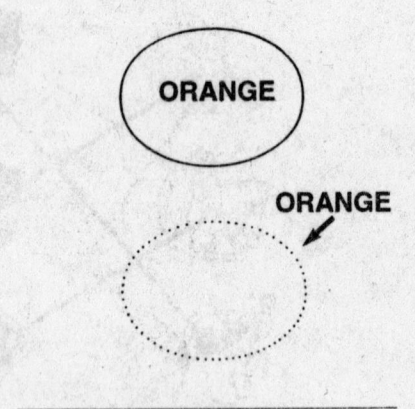

ORANGE

ORANGE

Page 14
Can you color the top diamond in purple?
Can you trace the bottom diamond in purple?
Can you find something purple or something that is a diamond?

PURPLE

PURPLE

©1998 Fisher-Price, Inc.

ANSWER KEY

Page 15
Can you color the top star in brown?
Can you trace the bottom star in brown?
Can you find something brown or something that is a star?

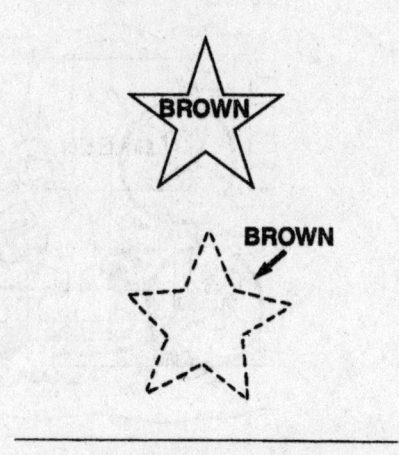

Page 17
Can you match the shapes that look the same?
Can you find matching shapes around you?

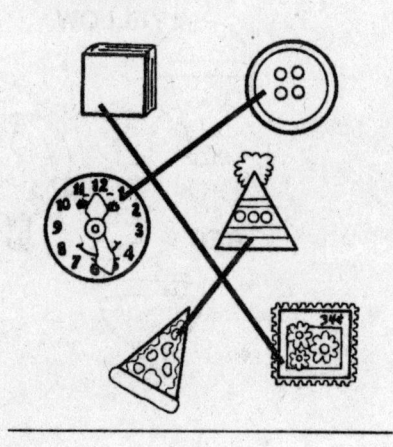

Page 18
Can you count to 10 and follow the dots?
Then color the picture.
Can you clap your hands 10 times?

Page 20
Can you name the letters and follow the dots?
Then color the picture.
Can you name each letter?

Page 21
Can you name the letters starting with N and follow the dots?
Then color the picture.
Can you name each letter?

Page 23
Can you tell what this picture really shows?
Then color the pictures.
Can you draw a picture and cut it up to make a puzzle?

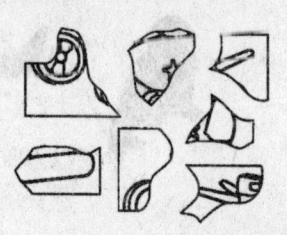

©1998 Fisher-Price, Inc.

ANSWER KEY

Page 24
Can you tell what this picture really shows?
Then color the pictures.
Can you cut up a magazine picture to make a puzzle?

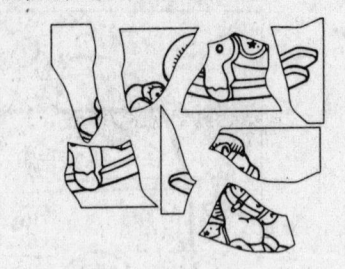

Page 25
Can you color the picture that takes more time to do?
Can you think of something that takes a long time to do?

Page 27
Can you remember the animals from the last page?
Color the ones you remember.
Can you close your eyes and remember what you are wearing?

Page 29
Can you circle someone holding a baby?
Can you circle someone holding a leash?
Then color the picture.
Can you find a kitten?

Page 30
Can you color the highest balloon **yellow**?
Can you color the lowest balloon **red**?
Can you color the balloon in the middle **blue**?

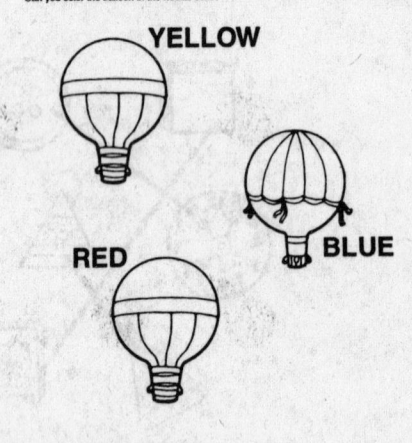

YELLOW
RED   BLUE

Page 31
Can you circle the acorn at the **top**?
Can you draw a line under the acorn at the **bottom**?
Can you color the acorn in the **middle**?
What animals live in a tree?

©1998 Fisher-Price, Inc.

46

ANSWER KEY

Page 32
Can you match the blocks that show the same letters?
Then color the picture.
Can you name the shapes of each block?

Page 33
Can you color the fruits that show the same letters?
Can you name other kinds of fruits?

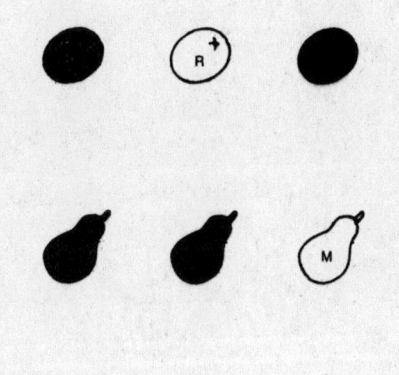

Page 34
Can you color the vegetables that show the same letters?
Can you name other kinds of vegetables?

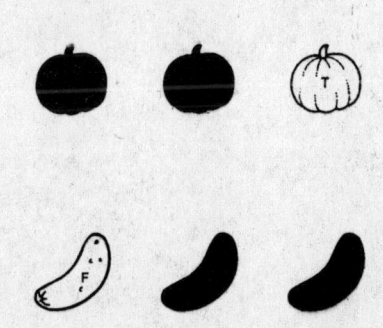

Page 35
Can you color the leaves that show the same letters?
Can you pretend to be a falling leaf?

Page 37
Can you color the matching number of things in each row?
Where could you use these things?

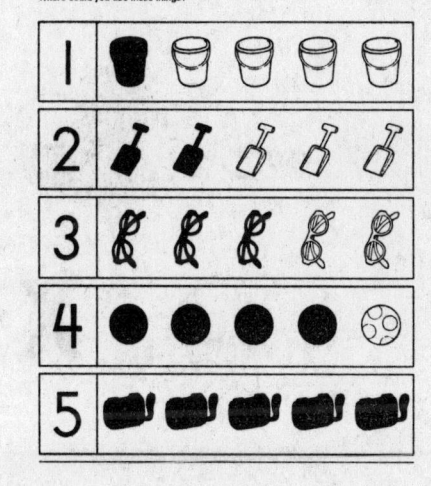

Page 38
Can you color the matching number of things in each row?
Where could you find these things in your home?

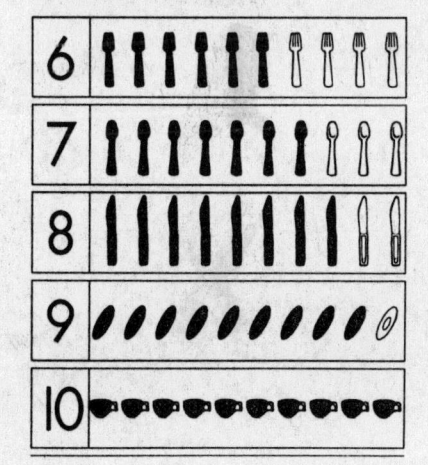

©1998 Fisher-Price, Inc.

ANSWER KEY

Page 39 Can you circle all the numbers?
Can you count to 5?

Page 40 Can you mark the one that doesn't belong?
Then color the other pictures.
Why do they go together?

Page 41 Can you mark the one that doesn't belong?
Then color the other pictures.
Why do they go together?

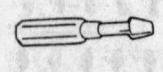

©1998 Fisher-Price, Inc.